June 2013

MILITARY BASES

DOD Has Processes to Comply with Statutory Requirements for Closing or Realigning Installations

GAO Highlights

Highlights of GAO-13-645, a report to congressional committees

MILITARY BASES

DOD Has Processes to Comply with Statutory Requirements for Closing or Realigning Installations

Why GAO Did This Study

DOD may be required to meet specific statutory requirements before closing or realigning installations that are authorized to employ 300 or more DOD civilians. In light of these requirements, DOD has historically used the BRAC process for closing or realigning bases that are above statutory thresholds. However, in March 2012, the Deputy Under Secretary of Defense (Installations and Environment) testified that because of fiscal and strategic imperatives, in the absence of an additional BRAC round, DOD may be forced to use its existing authorities to begin to realign and close bases. Subsequently, the National Defense Authorization Act for Fiscal Year 2013 mandated GAO to review the processes that DOD uses to close and realign military installations outside of the BRAC process. This report describes the extent to which DOD has processes in place to implement installation closures and realignments within the United States, and the extent to which DOD has implemented closures and realignments outside of the BRAC process.

To conduct its work, GAO examined DOD's approach to implementing basing actions and interviewed DOD officials to identify how their approach ensures compliance with 10 U.S.C. § 2687.

GAO is not making any recommendations in this report. In commenting on this report DOD stated the report, in general, explains the processes it follows to comply with requirements for closing or realigning installations outside of a congressionally authorized BRAC process.

View GAO-13-645. For more information, contact Brian Lepore at (202) 512-4523 or leporeb@gao.gov.

What GAO Found

The Department of Defense (DOD) and the military services have processes to meet statutory requirements for base closures and realignments, and use these processes hundreds of times each year to make basing decisions outside of the Base Realignment and Closure (BRAC) process. These processes provide guidance for all types of basing actions, including, but not limited to base closures and realignments. For example, basing decisions can include actions such as reductions in force, disestablishments, renaming a command, and other organization changes. Generally, each service's basing decision process uses similar criteria, scope, and methodologies to determine where to locate its force structure, and each process is documented in established guidance. Each service's process requires a series of analyses, such as analysis of capability and capacity, cost estimates, and environmental considerations. Additionally, each service basing decision process includes legal reviews and an evaluation of the effect on civilian personnel. According to service officials, these reviews provide them data to determine whether a closure or realignment is above thresholds established in section 2687 of Title 10, U.S. Code (hereafter 10 U.S.C. § 2687), and therefore subject to additional evaluations and congressional notification. Specific statutory thresholds include:

- closure of any installation with 300 or more direct-hire DOD civilian authorized positions (this includes all authorized positions, regardless of whether they are vacant or filled); and

- realignment of any installation with 300 or more direct-hire DOD civilian authorized positions (vacant or filled), if the realignment will reduce the installation by 1,000 or more civilian positions, or 50 percent or more of the total civilian authorized positions.

DOD has conducted closures or realignments that have either fallen below the thresholds of 10 U.S.C. § 2687 or were authorized by the BRAC process, according to DOD officials. For example, the January 2011 disestablishment of Joint Forces Command was a basing decision that, according to DOD, reduced civilian personnel and eliminated functions at multiple installations, but did not require evaluations and congressional notification pursuant to 10 U.S.C. § 2687. Specifically, one of the installations affected by the disestablishment of Joint Forces Command was Naval Support Activity Norfolk, Virginia—the installation where Joint Forces Command was headquartered. Naval Support Activity Norfolk had approximately 3,200 civilian personnel at the time of the disestablishment, of which 1,058 (about 33 percent) were Joint Forces Command personnel. According to DOD, a significant number of Joint Forces Command functions and positions were eliminated through a reduction in force—an action that is not subject to 10 U.S.C. § 2687—and the remainder were part of a realignment of Naval Support Activity Norfolk that fell below the statutory thresholds of 1,000 authorized civilian personnel or 50 percent of the total civilian personnel authorized to be employed at the installation. Officials also told us they do not anticipate any future closures or realignments pursuant to this statute, citing BRAC as the preferred method for implementing basing actions that are above statutory thresholds.

_____ United States Government Accountability Office

Contents

Abbreviations

BRAC	base realignment and closure
DOD	Department of Defense
OSD	Office of the Secretary of Defense

June 27, 2013

Congressional Committees

The military services' decisions about where to base their force structure in the United States can have significant strategic, socioeconomic, and cost implications for the Department of Defense (DOD) and affected communities. In 1977, Congress passed legislation requiring DOD to meet specific requirements before closing or realigning installations that are authorized to employ a certain number of DOD civilians.[1] These statutory requirements, found at section 2687 of title 10, U.S. Code (hereafter 10 U.S.C. § 2687), have, according to DOD officials, constrained their ability to close or realign installations exceeding the civilian personnel thresholds. DOD has instead used the Base Realignment and Closure (BRAC) process since its enactment for these purposes. In March 2012, the Deputy Under Secretary of Defense (Installations and Environment) testified that because of fiscal and strategic imperatives, in the absence of congressional authorization for an additional BRAC round, DOD may be "forced to use its existing authorities to begin to realign and close bases."[2] Subsequently, in the National Defense Authorization Act for Fiscal Year 2013,[3] Congress mandated GAO to review the processes that DOD uses to make decisions relating to closures and realignments at military installations, including closures and realignments occurring both above and below the threshold levels specified in 10 U.S.C. § 2687. This report describes the extent to which DOD has processes in place to implement installation closures and realignments within the United States, and the extent to which DOD has implemented closures and realignments outside of the BRAC process. For a copy of the full language of 10 U.S.C. § 2687, see appendix I.

---

[1]Pub. L. No. 95-82, § 612 (1977).

[2]*Hearing on the Request for Authorization of Another BRAC Round and Additional Reductions in Overseas Bases, Before the Readiness Subcommittee of the House Committee on Armed Services*, 112th Cong. 38 (Mar. 8, 2012) (testimony of Under Secretary of Defense (Installations and Environment) Dr. Dorothy Robyn).

[3]Pub. L. No. 112-239, § 2712 (2013).

The scope of our work was to provide a description of the processes used by DOD in making decisions to close or realign military installations within the United States (50 states, the District of Columbia, and U.S. territories), pursuant to 10 U.S.C. § 2687. To determine the extent to which DOD has processes in place for closing and realigning military installations outside of the BRAC process, we identified and examined current DOD processes for implementing basing actions.[4] To determine whether the services' processes include steps to ensure compliance with the requirements of 10 U.S.C. § 2687, we reviewed documents and discussed the processes with officials in the Office of the Secretary of Defense (OSD) and each of the services to identify when and where in the processes' closures and realignments are reviewed for compliance with the statute. Furthermore, we met with attorneys from the Office of General Counsel in OSD and each of the services to discuss their interpretations of the statute and how these interpretations may affect DOD's ability to ensure consistent compliance with 10 U.S.C. § 2687. To describe the extent to which each service has closed or realigned installations pursuant to 10 U.S.C. § 2687, we met with officials and reviewed data from each of the services related to all basing actions affecting civilian personnel during fiscal years 2009 through 2012. Additionally, because some requirements in 10 U.S.C. § 2687 were enacted as recently as January 2013, and may not yet be reflected in the services' processes, for these requirements we reviewed the steps DOD is taking to update its processes to ensure compliance with the new requirements.[5]

We conducted this performance audit from November 2012 to June 2013 in accordance with generally accepted government auditing standards. Those standards require that we plan and perform the audit to obtain sufficient, appropriate evidence to provide a reasonable basis for our findings and conclusions based on our audit objectives. We believe that the evidence obtained provides a reasonable basis for our findings and conclusions based on our audit objectives.

---

[4]The four military services each use different terminology and definitions when describing their basing decision processes. For example, the Army describes its process as "stationing," the Marine Corps generally uses the term "force laydown," the Air Force uses the term "beddown," and the Navy uses the terms "strategic laydown" and "strategic dispersal." For the purposes of this report, we use "basing" to refer to the services' processes to make decisions about where to establish locations for their force structure.

[5]Pub.L. No. 112-239, § 2712 (2013).

Background

In the early 1960s, the Secretary of Defense, at the President's direction, developed and implemented a base closure program, with minimal consultation with Congress. This program resulted in hundreds of base closures and realignments, including closure of more than 60 major bases. Subsequently, in 1977, Congress enacted 10 U.S.C. § 2687 to establish procedures that DOD must generally follow when closing or realigning a military installation, in the United States or its territories, where 500 or more civilian personnel were authorized to be employed.[6] In 1978, Congress amended the law by lowering the threshold to 300 or more civilian personnel.[7] In the years following the passage of 10 U.S.C. § 2687, DOD's attempts to close major installations in the United States did not succeed. Consequently, in 1988 the Secretary of Defense chartered the first BRAC Commission to review and recommend bases for realignment and closure.[8] In 1990, Congress revised the BRAC process, which has, as amended, governed subsequent rounds of realignments and closures in 1991, 1993, 1995, and 2005.[9] Most recently, in its proposed budget for fiscal year 2014, DOD requested authorization for an additional BRAC round.

In the absence of authorization to carry out the BRAC process, installation closures and realignments that are subject to the requirements in 10 U.S.C. § 2687 include the

- closure of any installation with 300 or more direct-hire permanent DOD civilian authorized positions (this includes all authorized positions, regardless of whether they are vacant or filled); and
- realignment of any installation with 300 or more direct-hire permanent DOD civilian authorized positions (vacant or filled), if the realignment

---

[6]10 U.S.C. § 2687 applies to any military installation that is located within any of the 50 States, the District of Columbia, the Commonwealth of Puerto Rico, American Samoa, the Virgin Islands, the Commonwealth of the Northern Mariana Islands, or Guam.

[7]Pub. L. No. 95-356, § 805 (1978).

[8]In 1988, the Secretary of Defense chartered the first BRAC Commission, which operated in accordance with the processes later established by Congress in the Defense Authorization Amendments and Base Closure and Realignment Act of 1988, Pub. L. No. 100-526 (1988).

[9]The 1990 statute, Pub. L. No. 101-510, Title XXIX (10 U.S.C. § 2687 note), authorized the 1991, 1993, and 1995 rounds. It has been amended numerous times, most significantly when Congress authorized BRAC 2005 with the passage of the National Defense Authorization Act for Fiscal Year 2002, Pub. L. No. 107-107, Title XXX (2001).

will involve a reduction by (1) 1,000 or more civilian positions, or (2) 50 percent or more of the total civilian authorized positions.[10]

Statutory requirements for closures or realignments exceeding these thresholds generally include, but are not limited to, congressional committee notification by the Secretary of Defense or military department Secretary of the proposed closure or realignment as part of its annual request for authorization of appropriations, and an evaluation of the fiscal, local economic, budgetary, environmental, strategic, and operational consequences of the closure or realignment. Additionally, in January 2013, 10 U.S.C. § 2687 was amended so as to prohibit closures and realignments at installations with fewer than 300 authorized DOD civilian personnel for 5 years after the date on which a decision is made to reduce the civilian personnel below 300.[11] Figure 1 provides a general overview of the requirements in 10 U.S.C. § 2687.

---

[10]See table 1 for a full definition of these statutory terms, and a summary of how DOD interprets them.

[11]Pub. L. No. 112-239, § 2712 (2013).

Figure 1: Overview of Closures and Realignments Pursuant to 10 U.S.C. § 2687

Closure

Does the installation to be closed have 300 or more authorized DOD civilian positions?

— Yes → **Closure**
This closure cannot proceed unless the Secretary concerned meets the congressional notification and reporting requirements of 10 U.S.C. § 2687(b) as part of an annual request for authorization of appropriations.

— No →

Has the installation been subject to a decision to reduce authorized civilian personnel below stated thresholds?

— Yes → Actions to close are prohibited for 5 years from the time the decision to reduce personnel was made.

— No → **Closure is not subject to 10 USC §2687**
If installation has fewer than 300 authorized DOD civilian positions, generally the services can make closure decisions at their discretion in accordance with other applicable laws and policies.

Realignment

Does the installation to be realigned have 300 or more authorized DOD civilian positions?

— No → Has the installation been subject to a decision to reduce authorized civilian personnel below stated thresholds?

— Yes (from that box) → Actions to realign that exceed stated thresholds are prohibited for 5 years from the time the decision to reduce personnel was made.

— No (from that box) → Action may be taken without congressional notification and evaluations required by 10 USC §2687. Action may still be subject to congressional notification per DOD policies, as well as other statutory requirements.

— Yes → Does the number of civilian personnel positions to be reduced at losing installation exceed
• 1,000 positions, or
• 50% of the total number of authorized DOD civilian personnel positions at the losing installation?

— No → (to "Action may be taken without congressional notification...")

— Yes → Does the action both reduce and relocate functions and civilian personnel positions to a new installation?

— No → **Action is not considered realignment as defined by 10 USC §2687**
If action does not meet both criteria, generally the services can make realignment decisions at their discretion in accordance with other applicable laws and policies.

— Yes → **Realignment**
This realignment cannot proceed unless the Secretary concerned meets the congressional notification and reporting requirements of 10 U.S.C. § 2687(b) as part of an annual request for authorization of appropriations.

Source: GAO summary of the process for closures and realignments under 10 U.S.C. § 2687

Table 1 provides a summary of the definitions of key terms included in the statute and DOD's interpretation of these terms.

Table 1: Key Terms Included in 10 U.S.C. § 2687 and Summary of DOD's Interpretation of Terms

Term	Definitions provided in 10 U.S.C. § 2687	Summary of DOD's interpretations of key terms
Civilian Personnel	Direct-hire, permanent civilian employees of the Department of Defense (DOD).	DOD officials we met with all agreed that temporary, term, or contract employees should not be counted towards the civilian personnel thresholds. Some officials we met with disagreed as to whether to include or exclude nonappropriated fund positions. Additionally, according to OSD officials any conclusion of the OSD General Counsel on this matter would be determinative.
Closure	The statute does not define what constitutes a closure.	In the absence of a definition for the term closure, the Office of the Secretary of Defense (OSD) has deferred to the definition of closure used in the BRAC process. DOD and prior BRAC Commissions have defined a "closure" as "all missions or activities of a certain installation have ceased or have been relocated. All personnel positions will either be eliminated or relocated, except for personnel required for caretaking, conducting any ongoing environmental cleanup and disposal of the base, or remaining in authorized enclaves."
Realignment	Any action which both reduces and relocates functions and civilian personnel positions, but does not include a reduction in force resulting from workload adjustments, reduced personnel or funding levels, skill imbalances, or other similar causes.	DOD officials interpret the term realignment to mean that authorized civilian positions are eliminated at the losing installation and moved during the relocation of a function to another installation. This may or may not result in an overall net loss of DOD civilian positions.
Military Installations	Refers to a base, camp, post, station, yard, center, homeport facility for any ship, or other activity under the jurisdiction of DOD including any leased facility, which is located within any of the several States, the District of Columbia, the Commonwealth of Puerto Rico, American Samoa, the Virgin Islands, the Commonwealth of the Northern Mariana Islands, or Guam. It does not include any facility used primarily for civil works, rivers and harbors projects, or flood control projects.	DOD officials agree the statutory definition of military installation is clear. While every discreet parcel of property could be viewed as a separate installation, it is standard practice in the military departments to assign smaller parcels of property, particularly leased property, to a nearby military installation, making that property part of the larger installation.

Source: 10 U.S.C. § 2687 and GAO summary of DOD information.

DOD Has Processes in Place for Making All Basing Decisions, Including Those Related to 10 U.S.C. § 2687, and Uses Them Hundreds of Time Per Year

DOD and the military services have processes in place to meet statutory requirements for basing decisions, and according to DOD officials they use these processes to make hundreds of basing decisions each year that are not subject to 10 U.S.C. § 2687. For example, in addition to closures and realignments, basing decisions can include actions such as reductions in force, disestablishments, changes to mission statements, and other organization changes. According to DOD officials, since the 1977 enactment of 10 U.S.C. § 2687, the department has not closed or realigned any installation pursuant to the procedures set out in 10 U.S.C. § 2687. All closures or realignments since 1977 have either fallen below the thresholds of 10 U.S.C. § 2687 or were undertaken with a statutorily authorized BRAC process. They also told us they do not anticipate that closures or realignments pursuant to this statute will take place in the near future, citing BRAC as the preferred method for implementing basing actions that are above statutory thresholds.

DOD Has Processes in Place for Making Basing Decisions That Comply with 10 U.S.C. § 2687

Each military service has its own processes for evaluating and implementing basing decisions, including proposals to close or realign installations outside of the BRAC process.[12] Generally, the services' basing decision processes use similar criteria, scope, and methodologies to determine where to locate the services' force structure, and each process is documented in established guidance. Each service's process requires a series of analyses, such as analysis of capability and capacity, cost estimates, and environmental considerations. For example, the Army's process includes publishing a comprehensive strategy, developing feasible alternatives, ensuring that the documentation of alternatives addresses all known costs, informing interested parties of actions, and obtaining decisions and clearance from Army headquarters to announce and execute any actions. Examples of criteria used by Army planners when developing feasible stationing alternatives include operational

---

[12]In May 2010, we issued a report evaluating the services' basing decision processes and we found that the processes used by the Army, Marine Corps, and Air Force fully incorporated the key elements, associated factors, and management-control standards that were necessary for a comprehensive process. We found that the Navy needed additional guidance for its processes to be complete, specifically that some of the Navy's guidance lacked detailed information about specific actions taken during the process and defining responsibility for completing certain types of analyses. According to Navy officials, steps are being taken to remedy these issues, and officials expect to issue revised guidance in fall 2013. GAO, *Defense Infrastructure: Opportunities Exist to Improve the Navy's Basing Decision Process and DOD Oversight,* GAO-10-482 (Washington, D.C.: May 11, 2010).

considerations, budget impact, facilities impact, and environmental impact. Similarly, the Air Force has a centralized basing process that includes the use of quantitative criteria in basing decisions such as mission imperatives, environmental effects, costs, and logistic support.

Each service's process also provides for a review of how decisions may affect civilian personnel. According to service officials, this review provides them with data to determine whether the basing action is above or below 10 U.S.C. § 2687 thresholds. Table 2 describes each military service's guidance and the requirements to evaluate any effect on civilian personnel.

Table 2: Civilian Personnel Data Required by Each Service in Making Basing Decisions

Service	Guidance document	Requirement to evaluate effect on civilian personnel
Air Force	Air Force Instruction 10-503, *Strategic Basing* Air Force Instruction 38-101, *Manpower and Organization*	Basing action requests require information on authorized and proposed staffing, including civilians.
Army	Army Regulation 5-10, *Stationing*	Basing actions require documentation of civilian impact, and the reduction in force or transfer of 50 or more civilians outside of the local commuting area requires additional actions to be taken, such as congressional notification and coordinating with the Civilian Human Resources Agency.
Marine Corps	Marine Corps Order 5311.1D, *Total Force Structure Process*	Basing actions include assessment to determine effects on civilian personnel.
Navy	Chief of Naval Operations Instruction 5400.44A, *Navy Organization Change Manual*	Basing actions require information on the effect of the action on civilian personnel, including the total number of civilian personnel and the total annual salary.

Source: GAO review of DOD documents.

In addition to the requirement to provide data on the effect on civilian personnel, each service's basing decision process includes legal reviews of basing decisions, which, according to service officials, occur at multiple stages throughout the process and ensure compliance with 10 U.S.C. § 2687 as well as all other applicable laws and policies. Service attorneys told us that during reviews of basing actions, if compliance questions arise there is coordination with OSD attorneys to ensure decisions are consistent across the services and comply with all applicable laws. For example, according to officials, service and OSD attorneys are currently discussing how to interpret a provision added to 10 U.S.C. § 2687 in January 2013 that states that no action may be taken to close or realign a military installation within 5 years after the date on which a decision is made to reduce the authorized civilian personnel at that installation below 300. On the basis of our interviews with service and OSD attorneys, there are variations in how to interpret this provision. In the view of OSD and Air Force officials, the new provision is retrospective—that is, any closure or realignment occurring after January 2013 would need to be evaluated to determine whether a service had taken action to reduce civilian positions below the threshold during the previous 5 years. Conversely, Army, Navy, and Marine Corps officials interpret the statute as prospective—that is, if any installation after January 2013 reduces its civilians below 300, DOD is prohibited from closing or realigning that installation for the next 5 years. At the time of our review OSD officials said that they were informally discussing the statute with the services as it relates to proposed realignments and closures; however, OSD officials stated that they have no immediate plans to issue clarifying guidance and stated that generally they play a minimal role in determining how the services manage their organizational needs through basing actions.[13]

DOD Makes Hundreds of Basing Decisions Annually

While 10 U.S.C. § 2687 establishes congressional notification and waiting-period requirements that DOD must meet when implementing closures or certain realignments, DOD may close or realign installations without being subject to those requirements if the proposed action falls below specific thresholds. Specifically, closures and realignments that trigger congressional notification and waiting include any:

- closure of any installation with 300 or more direct-hire permanent DOD civilian authorized positions (this includes all authorized positions, regardless of whether they are vacant or filled); or

- realignment of any installation with 300 or more direct-hire permanent DOD civilian authorized positions (vacant or filled), if the realignment will involve a reduction by (1) 1,000 or more civilian positions, or (2) 50 percent or more of the total civilian authorized positions.

According to service officials, they undertake hundreds of basing actions each year that do not trigger the requirements in 10 U.S.C. § 2687 because either they do not exceed the thresholds established in the

---

[13]According to OSD officials, they are only involved in the implementation of basing actions if there is a specific reason, such as for basing actions into or within the National Capital Region that exceed $500,000. These actions are restricted by law unless the Secretary of Defense waives the restriction by certifying in writing to the congressional defense committees that such a relocation is required in the best interest of the government.

statute, or the action does not qualify as a realignment as defined by the statue. During discussions with OSD and the military services, officials provided some examples of recent realignments that DOD determined were not subject to 10 U.S.C. § 2687. Below we describe three of these examples, which were selected because they demonstrate typical basing actions that are not subject to 10 U.S.C. § 2687.

The Disestablishment of the Joint Forces Command

The January 2011 disestablishment of Joint Forces Command led to approved basing decisions that, according to DOD, reduced civilian personnel and eliminated functions at multiple installations, but did not exceed the personnel threshold of 10 U.S.C. § 2687, which would have triggered the congressional notification and evaluation process. For example, one of the installations affected by the disestablishment of Joint Forces Command was Naval Support Activity Norfolk, Virginia—the installation where Joint Forces Command was headquartered. Naval Support Activity Norfolk, according to DOD documents, had approximately 3,200 civilian personnel at the time of the disestablishment, of which 1,058 (about 33 percent) were Joint Forces Command personnel.[14] According to DOD, a significant number of Joint Forces Command functions and positions were eliminated through a reduction in force—an action that is not subject to 10 U.S.C. § 2687—and the remainder were part of a realignment of Naval Support Activity Norfolk, which fell below the statutory thresholds of 1,000 authorized civilian personnel or 50 percent of the total civilian personnel authorized to be employed at the installation.

The Relocation of an Army Office from Tobyhanna Army Depot to Scott Air Force Base

The April 2012 relocation of the Army Intermodal Distribution Platform Management Office from the Tobyhanna Army Depot in Pennsylvania to the Scott Air Force Base in Illinois is another example of an approved basing decision that, according to DOD, did not exceed the personnel thresholds in 10 U.S.C. § 2687. This example demonstrates what the services characterize as a typical realignment. In this example, the Army made a decision—on the basis of an Army Audit Agency report—to relocate the Army Intermodal Distribution Platform Management Office and 14 of its authorized civilian positions from Tobyhanna Army Depot to Scott Air Force Base. At the time, Tobyhanna was authorized to employ

---

[14]Of the 1,058 Joint Forces Command civilian personnel, 516 were physically located within the Naval Support Activity Norfolk perimeter and 542 were at the Suffolk Annex, a leased location which, although located outside of the Naval Support Activity Norfolk perimeter, is considered part of Naval Support Activity Norfolk.

over 5,000 civilian personnel, making it potentially subject to compliance with the procedures of 10 U.S.C. § 2687. Additionally, this action would both reduce and relocate functions and civilian personnel positions, thereby meeting the definition of realignment established in 10 U.S.C. § 2687. However, because only 14 civilian authorizations (less than 1 percent of the total positions at the installation) were eliminated from Tobyhanna as a result of this action, and therefore did not exceed the 10 U.S.C. § 2687 threshold, the Army was not required to conduct evaluations and submit congressional notifications pursuant to 10 U.S.C. § 2687.

Consolidation of a Navy Mission from Norfolk, Virginia, at Newport, Rhode Island

The October 2011 disestablishment of the Center for Naval Engineering in Norfolk, Virginia, and the consolidation of its mission at the Surface Warfare Officers School Command in Newport, Rhode Island, is another example of an approved basing decision that, according to DOD, did not exceed the thresholds in 10 U.S.C. § 2687. This example demonstrates a realignment involving few authorized civilian personnel positions. As a result, the Navy disestablished the Center for Naval Engineering in Norfolk and seven civilian authorized positions were reduced. These authorizations accounted for less than 1 percent of the over 13,000 authorized civilian positions at Norfolk, and therefore did not exceed the 10 U.S.C. § 2687 threshold.

In discussing examples of basing actions, DOD officials stated that determining the total number of DOD civilian authorized positions at an installation can be challenging. Specifically, because each service maintains personnel data in different data systems, and because multiple services can be tenants at a single installation, it can be difficult to determine the total number of DOD authorized civilian positions. According to service officials, generally the service initiating the realignment will request the tenant organizations to provide the service with the total number of authorized civilian personnel located at the installation in question. For example, according to an OSD attorney, obtaining civilian personnel data for the Joint Forces Command disestablishment was an arduous process because the services and organizations within the services each have various systems and processes maintaining the necessary data. While collecting these data for Joint Forces Command was not easy, according to the OSD attorney responsible for reviewing the decision, she nonetheless was able to collect the necessary civilian personnel data to ensure compliance with 10 U.S.C. § 2687.

Further, we found that the services use caution when considering a basing action at an installation where the total number of personnel falls close to the 300-position threshold. For example, in February 2012, the Air Force considered a proposal to close the Air Reserve Station in Pittsburgh, Pennsylvania. According to an Air Force attorney, the Air Force determined that there were approximately 280 DOD authorized civilian positions at the Air Reserve Station, some of which were vacant. Because this number was close to the threshold established in 10 U.S.C. § 2687, additional steps were taken to ensure that the proposed closure would comply with the law. Specifically, in addition to the total number of authorized civilian positions, officials also determined the number of civilian over-hires[15] at the installation and included these in their count of authorized civilian personnel. While Air Force analysis determined that the overall number of authorized civilian personnel, including over-hires, was still fewer than 300, Air Force officials ultimately decided not to close the Air Reserve Station in Pittsburgh. Instead, according to officials, the Air Force plans on using the Air Reserve Station to house additional aircraft.

While these examples did not exceed the threshold requiring evaluations and congressional notification under 10 U.S.C. § 2687, DOD and the services have established requirements for congressional notification of planned basing actions. For example, the Marine Corps' process states that its Office of Legislative Affairs should keep Congress advised as appropriate of all changes associated with reorganizations. The Army's guidance provides that some members of Congress receive notice of approved basing actions before they are announced to the public, and in cases that DOD deems to be politically sensitive, members of Congress may be informed about a basing study that is being initiated at the time of the study's initiation. Additionally, a 2011 DOD instruction requires notice to Congress of decisions that, among other things, include the release of 50 or more civilian employees from federal employment during a fiscal year at an installation, facility, or activity; a closure or reduction in workforce at an installation that may be expected to be of interest to

---

[15]According to Air Force officials, when funding is available, units sometimes hire personnel for positions not reflected on the Unit Manning Document. These positions are called "over-hires."

GAO-13-645 Military Bases

members of Congress and the public; or the realignment of 50 or more civilian employees outside of the local commuting area.[16]

Agency Comments and Our Evaluation

We provided a draft of this report to DOD for comment. In its written comments, reproduced in appendix II, DOD stated this report, in general, explains the processes it follows to comply with requirements for closing or realigning installations outside of a congressionally authorized BRAC process. DOD also provided some technical comments. In response, we made editorial changes to specific sections of the report for clarity.

We are sending copies of this report to the appropriate congressional committees; the Secretary of Defense; the Secretaries of the Army, Navy, and Air Force and Commandant of the Marine Corps; and the Director, Office of Management and Budget. In addition, the report is available at no charge on the GAO website at http://www.gao.gov.

If you or your staff have any questions about this report, please contact me at (202) 512-4523 or leporeb@gao.gov. Contact points for our Offices of Congressional Relations and Public Affairs may be found on the last page of this report. GAO staff who made key contributions to this report are listed in appendix III.

Brian J. Lepore
Director
Defense Capabilities and Management

---

[16]Department of Defense, *DOD Civilian Personnel Management System: Coordination and Clearance Requirements for Personnel Reductions, Closures of Installations and Reductions of Contract Operations in the United States*, DOD Instruction 1400.25 (Jan. 19, 2011).

The Honorable Carl Levin
Chairman
The Honorable James M. Inhofe
Ranking Member
Committee on Armed Services
United States Senate

The Honorable Dick Durbin
Chairman
The Honorable Thad Cochran
Ranking Member
Subcommittee on Defense
Committee on Appropriations
United States Senate

The Honorable Tim Johnson
Chairman
The Honorable Mark Kirk
Ranking Member
Subcommittee on Military Construction, Veterans Affairs,
    and Related Agencies
Committee on Appropriations
United States Senate

The Honorable Howard P. "Buck" McKeon
Chairman
The Honorable Adam Smith
Ranking Member
Committee on Armed Services
House of Representatives

The Honorable Bill Young
Chairman
The Honorable Pete Visclosky
Ranking Member
Subcommittee on Defense
Committee on Appropriations
House of Representatives

The Honorable John Culberson
Chairman
The Honorable Sanford Bishop
Ranking Member
Subcommittee on Military Construction, Veterans Affairs,
    and Related Agencies
Committee on Appropriations
House of Representatives

Appendix I: 10 U.S.C. § 2687

(a) Notwithstanding any other provision of law, no action may be taken to effect or implement—

(1) the closure of any military installation at which at least 300 civilian personnel are authorized to be employed;

(2) any realignment with respect to any military installation referred to in paragraph
(1) involving a reduction by more than 1,000, or by more than 50 percent, in the number of civilian personnel authorized to be employed at such military installation at the time the Secretary of Defense or the Secretary of the military department concerned notifies the Congress under subsection (b) of the Secretary's plan to close or realign such installation; or

(3) any construction, conversion, or rehabilitation at any military facility other than a military installation referred to in clause (1) or (2) which will or may be required as a result of the relocation of civilian personnel to such facility by reason of any closure or realignment to which clause (1) or (2) applies, unless and until the provisions of subsection (b) are complied with.

(b) No action described in subsection (a) with respect to the closure of, or a realignment with respect to, any military installation referred to in such subsection may be taken unless and until—

(1) the Secretary of Defense or the Secretary of the military department concerned notifies the Committee on Armed Services of the Senate and the Committee on Armed Services of the House of Representatives, as part of an annual request for authorization of appropriations to such Committees, of the proposed closing or realignment and submits with the notification—

(A) an evaluation of the fiscal, local economic, budgetary, environmental, strategic, and operational consequences of such closure or realignment; and

(B) the criteria used to consider and recommend military installations for such closure or realignment, which shall include at a minimum consideration of—

(i) the ability of the infrastructure (including transportation infrastructure) of both the existing and receiving communities to support forces, missions, and personnel as a result of such closure or realignment; and

(ii) the costs associated with community transportation infrastructure improvements as part of the evaluation of cost savings or return on investment of such closure or realignment; and

(2) a period of 30 legislative days or 60 calendar days, whichever is longer, expires following the day on which the notice and evaluation referred to in clause (1) have been submitted to such committees, during which period no irrevocable action may be taken to effect or implement the decision.

(c) No action described in subsection (a) with respect to the closure of, or realignment with respect to, any military installation referred to in such subsection may be taken within five years after the date on which a decision is made to reduce the civilian personnel thresholds below the levels prescribed in such subsection.

(d) This section shall not apply to the closure of a military installation, or a realignment with respect to a military installation, if the President certifies to the Congress that such closure or realignment must be implemented for reasons of national security or a military emergency.

(e)(1) After the expiration of the period of time provided for in subsection (b)(2) with respect to the closure or realignment of a military installation, funds which would otherwise be available to the Secretary to effect the closure or realignment of that installation may be used by him for such purpose.

(2) Nothing in this section restricts the authority of the Secretary to obtain architectural and engineering services under section 2807 of this title.

(f) If the Secretary of Defense or the Secretary of the military department concerned determines, pursuant to the National Environmental Policy Act of 1969 (42 U.S.C. 4321 et seq.), that a significant transportation impact will occur as a result of an action described in subsection (a), the action may not be taken unless and until the Secretary of Defense or the Secretary of the military department concerned—

(1) analyzes the adequacy of transportation infrastructure at and in the vicinity of each military installation that would be impacted by the action;

(2) concludes consultation with the Secretary of Transportation with regard to such impact;

(3) analyzes the impact of the action on local businesses, neighborhoods, and local governments; and

(4) includes in the notification required by subsection (b)(1) a description of how the Secretary intends to remediate the significant transportation impact.

(g) In this section:

(1) The term "military installation" means a base, camp, post, station, yard, center, homeport facility for any ship, or other activity under the jurisdiction of the Department of Defense, including any leased facility, which is located within any of the several States, the District of Columbia, the Commonwealth of Puerto Rico, American Samoa, the Virgin Islands, the Commonwealth of the Northern Mariana Islands, or Guam. Such term does not include any facility used primarily for civil works, rivers and harbors projects, or flood control projects.

(2) The term "civilian personnel" means direct-hire, permanent civilian employees of the Department of Defense.

(3) The term "realignment" includes any action which both reduces and relocates functions and civilian personnel positions, but does not include a reduction in force resulting from workload adjustments, reduced personnel or funding levels, skill imbalances, or other similar causes.

(4) The term "legislative day" means a day on which either House of Congress is in session.

Appendix II: Comments from the Department of Defense

OFFICE OF THE UNDER SECRETARY OF DEFENSE
3000 DEFENSE PENTAGON
WASHINGTON, DC 20301-3000

ACQUISITION,
TECHNOLOGY
AND LOGISTICS

JUN 18 2013

Mr. Brian Lepore
Director, Defense Capabilities and Management
U.S. Government Accountability Office
441 G Street, N.W.
Washington, DC 20548

Dear Mr. Lepore:

    This is the Department of Defense (DoD) response to the GAO Draft Report 13-645, "MILITARY BASES: DoD Has Processes to Comply with Statutory Requirements for Closing or Realigning Installations," dated May 31, 2013 (GAO Code 351779).

    In general, the report explains the processes DoD follows to comply with requirements for closing or realigning installations outside of a congressionally authorized BRAC process. There are some corrections, however, that GAO must make to the report to accurately reflect the discussions that have occurred between our staffs and DoD's Office of General Counsel (see enclosed comments).

    We continue to appreciate the work of the GAO in its review of BRAC related issues.

Sincerely,

John Conger
Acting Deputy Under Secretary of Defense
(Installations and Environment)

Enclosure as stated

Note: Page numbers in
the draft report may differ
from those in this report.

Corrections for Draft Report GAO 13-645

GAO highlights page, second paragraph:

The sentence "According to DOD officials, since the enactment of 10 U.S.C. § 2687 in 1977 no
military installation has been closed outside of the BRAC process and realignments outside of
the BRAC process complied with 10 U.S.C. § 2687" is not an accurate reflection of discussions
with DoD. Rather, we said that since the enactment of 2687 in 1977, the Department has not
closed or realigned any installation pursuant to the procedures set out in 2687. All closures or
realignments since 1977 have either fallen below the thresholds of 2687 or were undertaken with
a statutorily authorized BRAC process.

Pg. 5 Table 1 Key Terms:

The Civilian Personnel line column two "Summary of DoD's interpretation of Key Terms"
would be made more accurate by adding a sentence such as "All DoD officials agreed, however,
that any conclusion of the OSD General Counsel on this matter would be determinative."

Pg. 6 top of the page first sentence:

The sentence "According to DOD officials, since the enactment of 10 U.S.C. § 2687 in 1977 no
military installation has been closed outside of the BRAC process and realignments outside of
the BRAC process have followed the established processes and complied with 10 U.S.C. §
2687," is not an accurate reflection of discussions with DoD. Rather, we said that since the
enactment of 2687 in 1977, the Department has not closed or realigned any installation pursuant
to the procedures set out in 2687. All closures or realignments since 1977 have either fallen
below the thresholds of 2687 or were undertaken with a statutorily authorized BRAC process.

Pg. 8 first full paragraph:

The sentence "While 10 U.S.C. § 2687 establishes Congressional notification and waiting period
requirements that DOD must meet when implementing closures or realignments of installations
with 300 or more authorized civilian positions, DOD has the authority to close or realign
installations that fall below this threshold without triggering the requirements" is accurate for
closures but not for realignments. Accordingly, suggest the sentence be rewritten to read as
follows:

"While 10 U.S.C. § 2687 establishes Congressional notification and waiting period requirements
that DoD must meet when implementing either closures of installations with 300 or more
authorized civilian positions or realignments of installations with 300 or more authorized civilian
positions if the realignment involves either 1000 civilian personnel positions or 50% of the
authorized civilian personnel positions, DoD has the authority to close or realign installations
that fall below these thresholds without triggering the requirements."

Appendix III: GAO Contact and Staff Acknowledgments

GAO Contact	Brian J. Lepore, (202) 512-4523 or leporeb@gao.gov
Staff Acknowledgments	In addition to the contact named above, Harold Reich (Assistant Director), Greg Marchand, Stephanie Moriarty, Richard Powelson, Tida Reveley, Kelly Rubin, and Amie Steele made key contributions to this report.

Related GAO Products

Defense Infrastructure: DOD's Excess Capacity Estimating Methods Have Limitations. GAO-13-535. Washington, D.C.: June 20, 2013.

Military Bases: Opportunities Exist to Improve Future Base Realignment and Closure Rounds. GAO-13-149. Washington, D.C.: March 7, 2013.

DOD Joint Bases: Management Improvements Needed to Achieve Greater Efficiencies. GAO-13-134. Washington, D.C.: November 15, 2012.

Military Base Realignments and Closures: The National Geospatial-Intelligence Agency's Technology Center Construction Project. GAO-12-770R. Washington, D.C.: June 29, 2012.

Military Base Realignments and Closures: Updated Costs and Savings Estimates from BRAC 2005. GAO-12-709R. Washington, D.C.: June 29, 2012.

Military Base Realignments and Closures: Key Factors Contributing to BRAC 2005 Results. GAO-12-513T. Washington, D.C.: March 8, 2012.

Excess Facilities: DOD Needs More Complete Information and a Strategy to Guide Its Future Disposal Efforts. GAO-11-814. Washington, D.C.: September 19, 2011.

Military Base Realignments and Closures: Review of the Iowa and Milan Army Ammunition Plants. GAO-11-488R. Washington, D.C.: April 1, 2011.

GAO's 2011 High-Risk Series: An Update. GAO-11-394T. Washington, D.C.: February 17, 2011.

Defense Infrastructure: High-Level Federal Interagency Coordination Is Warranted to Address Transportation Needs beyond the Scope of the Defense Access Roads Program. GAO-11-165. Washington, D.C.: January 26, 2011.

Military Base Realignments and Closures: DOD Is Taking Steps to Mitigate Challenges but Is Not Fully Reporting Some Additional Costs. GAO-10-725R. Washington, D.C.: July 21, 2010.

Defense Infrastructure: Army Needs to Improve Its Facility Planning Systems to Better Support Installations Experiencing Significant Growth. GAO-10-602. Washington, D.C.: June 24, 2010.

Military Base Realignments and Closures: Estimated Costs Have Increased While Savings Estimates Have Decreased Since Fiscal Year 2009. GAO-10-98R. Washington, D.C.: November 13, 2009.

Military Base Realignments and Closures: Transportation Impact of Personnel Increases Will Be Significant, but Long-Term Costs Are Uncertain and Direct Federal Support Is Limited. GAO-09-750. Washington, D.C.: September 9, 2009.

Military Base Realignments and Closures: DOD Needs to Update Savings Estimates and Continue to Address Challenges in Consolidating Supply-Related Functions at Depot Maintenance Locations. GAO-09-703. Washington, D.C.: July 9, 2009.

Defense Infrastructure: DOD Needs to Periodically Review Support Standards and Costs at Joint Bases and Better Inform Congress of Facility Sustainment Funding Uses. GAO-09-336. Washington, D.C.: March 30, 2009.

Military Base Realignments and Closures: DOD Faces Challenges in Implementing Recommendations on Time and Is Not Consistently Updating Savings Estimates. GAO-09-217. Washington, D.C.: January 30, 2009.

Military Base Realignments and Closures: Army Is Developing Plans to Transfer Functions from Fort Monmouth, New Jersey, to Aberdeen Proving Ground, Maryland, but Challenges Remain. GAO-08-1010R. Washington, D.C.: August 13, 2008.

Defense Infrastructure: High-Level Leadership Needed to Help Communities Address Challenges Caused by DOD-Related Growth. GAO-08-665. Washington, D.C.: June 17, 2008.

Defense Infrastructure: DOD Funding for Infrastructure and Road Improvements Surrounding Growth Installations. GAO-08-602R. Washington, D.C.: April 1, 2008.

Military Base Realignments and Closures: Higher Costs and Lower Savings Projected for Implementing Two Key Supply-Related BRAC Recommendations. GAO-08-315. Washington, D.C.: March 5, 2008.

Defense Infrastructure: Realignment of Air Force Special Operations Command Units to Cannon Air Force Base, New Mexico. GAO-08-244R. Washington, D.C.: January 18, 2008.

Military Base Realignments and Closures: Estimated Costs Have Increased and Estimated Savings Have Decreased. GAO-08-341T. Washington, D.C.: December 12, 2007.

Military Base Realignments and Closures: Cost Estimates Have Increased and Are Likely to Continue to Evolve. GAO-08-159. Washington, D.C.: December 11, 2007.

Military Base Realignments and Closures: Impact of Terminating, Relocating, or Outsourcing the Services of the Armed Forces Institute of Pathology. GAO-08-20. Washington, D.C.: November 9, 2007.

Military Base Realignments and Closures: Transfer of Supply, Storage, and Distribution Functions from Military Services to Defense Logistics Agency. GAO-08-121R. Washington, D.C.: October 26, 2007.

Defense Infrastructure: Challenges Increase Risks for Providing Timely Infrastructure Support for Army Installations Expecting Substantial Personnel Growth. GAO-07-1007. Washington, D.C.: September 13, 2007.

Military Base Realignments and Closures: Plan Needed to Monitor Challenges for Completing More Than 100 Armed Forces Reserve Centers. GAO-07-1040. Washington, D.C.: September 13, 2007.

Military Base Realignments and Closures: Observations Related to the 2005 Round. GAO-07-1203R. Washington, D.C.: September 6, 2007.

Military Base Closures: Projected Savings from Fleet Readiness Centers Likely Overstated and Actions Needed to Track Actual Savings and Overcome Certain Challenges. GAO-07-304. Washington, D.C.: June 29, 2007.

Military Base Closures: Management Strategy Needed to Mitigate Challenges and Improve Communication to Help Ensure Timely

Implementation of Air National Guard Recommendations. GAO-07-641. Washington, D.C.: May 16, 2007.

Military Base Closures: Opportunities Exist to Improve Environmental Cleanup Cost Reporting and to Expedite Transfer of Unneeded Property. GAO-07-166. Washington, D.C.: January 30, 2007.

Military Bases: Observations on DOD's 2005 Base Realignment and Closure Selection Process and Recommendations. GAO-05-905. Washington, D.C.: July 18, 2005.

Military Bases: Analysis of DOD's 2005 Selection Process and Recommendations for Base Closures and Realignments. GAO-05-785. Washington, D.C.: July 1, 2005.

Military Base Closures: Observations on Prior and Current BRAC Rounds. GAO-05-614. Washington, D.C.: May 3, 2005.

Military Base Closures: Assessment of DOD's 2004 Report on the Need for a Base Realignment and Closure Round. GAO-04-760. Washington, D.C.: May 17, 2004.

Military Bases: Review of DOD's 1998 Report on Base Realignment and Closure. GAO/NSIAD-99-17. Washington, D.C.: November 13, 1998.

GAO's Mission	The Government Accountability Office, the audit, evaluation, and investigative arm of Congress, exists to support Congress in meeting its constitutional responsibilities and to help improve the performance and accountability of the federal government for the American people. GAO examines the use of public funds; evaluates federal programs and policies; and provides analyses, recommendations, and other assistance to help Congress make informed oversight, policy, and funding decisions. GAO's commitment to good government is reflected in its core values of accountability, integrity, and reliability.
Obtaining Copies of GAO Reports and Testimony	The fastest and easiest way to obtain copies of GAO documents at no cost is through GAO's website (http://www.gao.gov). Each weekday afternoon, GAO posts on its website newly released reports, testimony, and correspondence. To have GAO e-mail you a list of newly posted products, go to http://www.gao.gov and select "E-mail Updates."
Order by Phone	The price of each GAO publication reflects GAO's actual cost of production and distribution and depends on the number of pages in the publication and whether the publication is printed in color or black and white. Pricing and ordering information is posted on GAO's website, http://www.gao.gov/ordering.htm. Place orders by calling (202) 512-6000, toll free (866) 801-7077, or TDD (202) 512-2537. Orders may be paid for using American Express, Discover Card, MasterCard, Visa, check, or money order. Call for additional information.
Connect with GAO	Connect with GAO on Facebook, Flickr, Twitter, and YouTube. Subscribe to our RSS Feeds or E-mail Updates. Listen to our Podcasts. Visit GAO on the web at www.gao.gov.
To Report Fraud, Waste, and Abuse in Federal Programs	Contact: Website: http://www.gao.gov/fraudnet/fraudnet.htm E-mail: fraudnet@gao.gov Automated answering system: (800) 424-5454 or (202) 512-7470
Congressional Relations	Katherine Siggerud, Managing Director, siggerudk@gao.gov, (202) 512-4400, U.S. Government Accountability Office, 441 G Street NW, Room 7125, Washington, DC 20548
Public Affairs	Chuck Young, Managing Director, youngc1@gao.gov, (202) 512-4800 U.S. Government Accountability Office, 441 G Street NW, Room 7149 Washington, DC 20548